MOTHER JACKSON MURDERS THE MOON

MOTHER JACKSON MURDERS THE MOON

GLORIA ESCOFFERY

PEEPAL TREE

First published in Great Britain in 1998
Peepal Tree Press Ltd
17 King's Avenue
Leeds LS6 1QS

ISBN 1 900715 24 4

CONTENTS

ROOTSMAN THEATRE OF THE ABSURD

THE LAPITHS

I: RITES OF SPRING

Cornhandman officiates as high priest
but Kiddo Karate performs the key ritual.
Aliveyah has been stepped over so often
she maintains the dignity of an upright posture
while seated splay-legged on the ground.
Not having been conditioned to the solace of literature
she hears in her heart
no echo of Milkwood Rosie's sleepy jug jug –
"Isn't life a terrible thing, thank God!"

II: ALIVEYAH AND THE TURTLEDOVES

Nature speaks to Aliveyah
direct by the nudge of a beak
in the region of her belly button.
She listens, and Spring happens for her
regardless of impertinent bystanders
like Monkey with his pink and blue
plastic ball bells.
For a time she dwells among waterfalls
bordered by the plumage of lizard cuckoos.

III: CARNIVAL

Before a backdrop of Caribe blue
the spectacle of Ash Sunday
is enacted on Easter Monday.
Tourists, being *non persona* in the eyes of the natives,
are absent from the documentary recording the festivities.
Bongo Lapith and Aliveyah mark the occasion
by discovering they were meant for each other.
He drums out his call of the wild
and she joyfully claims her trophy.
Nyah Lapith the envious, more she than he
in his secret being, presses up against Guitar Joe
and makes his pander presence felt.
In the general jubilation
every act of love is warmly tolerated.

IV: BACCHANALE

This is the climactic moment. Sabine Aliveyah
delights in being lifted up on high
by a Karate Machito grown so grand
in the esteem of the celebrants.
All have turned out – Nyah, Cornhand, Wangler,
Bongoman, Brother Moses, Guitar Joe, Machito,
and Mr Back-to-Front Anansi with his two faces,
to see the couple off on their ritual honeymoon
beyond the last, spirited range of hills.
How glorious is drunkenness!
It reminds the Lapiths
of their superiority over the Centaurs.

V: MEMENTO MORI

Trinidad licensed Derek Walcott
laureate of the penitential morning.
The pathos of human illusions,
the unquenchable fragrance of the wilting rose,
are themes too subtle for Dub Deacon Lapith.
Astride the skull of an ass he sits a-musing,
rolling on the tongue of his ear a brainbusting sermon.
His sankey soul transmits decibels of righteousness
powerful enough to smash Aliveyah,
whore of Babylon,
and blast the pagan shebang of the cavalcade
out of being...
its sole remainder a trail of ash.

VI: LAW AND ORDER

The phantom of Papillon
hovers over Devil's Island.
Moses Lapith plugs the mouth of the wine bottle
with one clubfoot.
He raises beseeching arms to heaven,
pleading for a new set of laws
chiselled in creole –
a word which sets on edge the teeth of the patois speakers.
The protesters huddle in what they hope
will be an effective road block.
Stalin Lapith mans the gun turret
combat station of his police vehicle.
Members of the Force who are closer to the ground
have gone off, backstage,
to organise the divvying up of the bread.

VII: HITEC

We are the legionnaires, the accredited
leg men despatched by our parliamentarians.
We voyage abroad in our seven-league boots
and model our manufacturers' carefree sandals on our heads.
This can not fail to create a sensation
in the cosmopolitan cosmos.
By graceful porterage of our samples
we honour our matriarchs.
Our headware may stink a little
but it is serviceable and flattering.
Jack Mandora, mix, max, fix, fax...
Who could resist such up-to-date subliminal
professionalism!

VIII: CONSPIRACY IN TWO ACTS

A Spanish jar consolidates the secret wishes
of four homunculi cogitating a contract.
This precious historic artefact
harbours more guilty secrets
than Grandma's closet houses cockroaches.
Where is Brutus?
In the company of this gang of four Cascas
no joker would have nerve enough
even to masquerade as a Brutus.
Et tu, Brute?
The retinal glint in the detached eye
of fallen Julius Lapith
is lively as a mess of slashed snakes.
He knows, the Generalissimo knows
the potency of incantation;
and the longevity of a profile
graven in coin of the realm.

IX: OLD TIME RELIGION

Bedward, alas, poor Bedward Lapith!
Every broken down bangarang
even prayers can't fix
must laugh at him,
come cockcrow countdown, stalled in macca tree
like kite on Easter Tuesday.
Truth to tell t'was Busha Godhead self
came swoopsing down,
handed out yellow card
and off again like breeze blow
to upper Empyrean.
It should have been red, some said.
Morning breeze brought bird, butterfly
and flying saucer out
to praise God and clap wings.
Facety nayger. boasting he could fly
and didn't try to help himself
with scandal bag paper and chicken wire –
just in case.

X: PATERFAMILIAS JONES

Peering out from his silver-plated cave
that is both cage and bomb shelter,
Jones Lapith, paterfamilias,
confronts the future with *savoir faire*.
Who but he would have thought of salvaging
that heirloom and relic of classier times,
Mother-in-law's silver tea urn?
Savaged by her in a moment of postnuptial experimentation
it had come to grief
in the melting pot of the coal pot.
The lid, severed but jauntily classic as ever,
provides a sunshade for Mr Jones.
Cooling beads of sweat saturate the Shakespearian
brow – and flavour the brew.
He experiences a sense of panic
which refuses to dissolve.
Where, nowadays, is there to be found a man of science
who can obliterate the tattooed D O N
visible on the chest of his son the Machitito?
Stolid as a flat-iron mahogany frog
carved by an intuitive, Madame Jones
conceals her envy of the neighbour's new backpack.
Who would not yearn to possess
such pachydermatous hand luggage!
What she covets most
is the personalised logo
craftily incised on the packy's exterior –
"Positive vibrations... EXODUS"

MOTHER JACKSON MURDERS THE MOON

Mother Jackson
sees the moon coming at her
and slams the door of her shack
so hard
the tin louvres shudder with eagerness
to let the moon in.
If she should cry for help
the dog would skin its teeth at her,
the cat would hoist its tail
and pin the whole moonlit sky to the gutter.
The neighbours would maybe
douse her in chicken blood
and hang her skin out to dry
on the packy tree.

Mother Jackson
swallows her bile and sprinkles oil
from the kitchen bitch on her ragged mattress.
Then she lights a firestick
and waits for the moon to take her.

HONEST MOTHER JACKSON

Mother Jackson
never lies – or so she says.
She lays her thoughts out
like an experienced mortician
while truth grins at her
from a nest in the cherry tree.
When she runs out of words
her old croaking lizard continues
to lay down the law of the wild
from his chink in the rafters.
Mother Jackson
never sleeps. All night long
she never once closes her eyes.
The flea that enlivens her dreams
knows better.
In the morning she hunts him down
and scrunches his fat belly with her thumb nails.

MOTHER JACKSON AND THE TOMATOES

Peering through the spider grill at the window
of the habitation she calls her own,
Mother Jackson levels with the lumpy, green tomatoes
pumping themselves up to maturity.
Distorted by the cataract crimp in her one serviceable eye,
they seem to cluster together in league against her.
She feels in her bones the chill of their self-containment,
interpreting it as a display of innocence, tinged with mockery.
The tightness of their pale, luminous skins
not yet primed to a blush
reminds her of her salad days –
taunting her with the green core-loneliness
of eighty unfulfilling years.
"Who sprinkled your seeds
row by row in an old seed box?" she breathes,
"and transplanted your brat suckers
in earth rich with cow dung reduced to dust?
Who dragged the garden boy's hose two chains to water you?
And had to nag the garden boy to fetch those ragged sticks
staked upright and firm in the loam for you to lean on?
Who stabbed one crooked finger teasing out a tangle of raffia,
and fumbled with stubborn knots, struggling
to anchor your limp stems to the crooksticks?
Who was it rescued you when your heads
of their own weight bowed to Mother Earth?"
The fruit, devoid of human affection or malice,
though it is well known that plants respond to music of sorts,
continue to burgeon in silence.
But it seems Mother Jackson derives solace
from the thoughts in her own head.
"I should have let you take your chances with the slugs,"
she adds, a note of tenderness creeping into her voice,
"and saved myself the expense of the insect spray."
From where she stands in her parlour, Mother Jackson

could squeeze one arm through the grill
to reach out and caress the frilly party dresses,
or count the fruit by touch, each on its splayed stalk.
She resists the temptation being mindful not to injure
the tender creatures she has nurtured.
The acrid scent of the plants fills her nostrils,
more health-giving than breath of peppermint or rosemary.

SERENADE

Who knows better than Bob Lapith, troubadour,
the secret springs of women's tears?
Like Antony he has clocked each sensual moment
in ordinals. Cardinal rigid in stone
his Roman heart is constant as an ice floe
towards his Octavian Aliveyah – and as cold.
"Husband, I come," sighs Antony's serpent of old Nile,
taking to breast the greedy asps.
Aliveyah, should she condescend to play the Cleopatra,
will rewrite the denouement.
She is a daughter of life's here and now
and will wear out her October
like an Arachne fabricating centrepieces.
The polished tables in her house
will rejoice in their adornment and
church fairs will provide an outlet for the surplus.
Ice cream cones for the children will
sunburst from her profitable superfluity.
In the beams of her home-sweet-home lamp
what gaudy filaments spring
from the fringes and fingers of her eyes,
what triumphant variations
transform the traditional crochet patterns!

IS WHO DAT I HEAR SAY CARNIVAL?

Farewell to flesh, carne vale, ain't
in Brudder-Back-to-Front-Anansi I-an'-I language.
Same time you yeye dazzle deh watch de black,
black-man-time-now
Johncunnoo black mask spin roun', spin roun'
tel it catch up wid de ol' time Johncunnoo white one,
same time Back-to-Front growl like empty belly
an' grin as if duppy eena him yeye corner.

A wha' dis poor-me-see-me-trial-now, you a go awn wid?
De soso ten cent gone from you pants pocket?
After is not you but one third cousin same name like you
(so you say) favour red man, fe true?
An' is you sister, not you, de fast man dem
a bad-name browning when she cut she yeye pon dem?
Fe you 'kin black, it black no johncrow you say?
In trut' me don' know weder to say shame on you or I sorry fe you.

Is Back-to-Front de street corner don dem did learn from, yah!
Which way two han' can match fe spider six?
Meantime one fe-you han reach out grab icecream cone fe suck,
de oder mek fe cover head gainst sun hot.
Well master, ef you tun stupid jus' like touris',
serve you right, me say.
An' ef you settle you mind fe ben' you back
an' tek straw mek brick, is fe you business yah.
Hones'-labour time done fe Brother-Back-to-Front,
an for all I-man like poor-me-bwoy too.
Chief Back-to-Front tun task master now,
fe-him guzzoo more potent when it come to catching
everybody same time
dan stupid-bakra-people-dem internet.

COCO THE CONTORTIONIST ADDRESSES HIS THOUGHTS TO THE ASSEMBLED WORSHIPPERS IN DIRIAMBO, NICARAGUA

If my legs were straight and rigid, my complexion
glaring white as the pilasters that guard
the welcoming porch of the church,
I would not now lie hunched beneath the hill
not even bothering to censure your feckless multitudes,
beguiling as the foetal nosegay on a lady's breast.
The statured saints assembled here for your January fiesta
seem to smile just as you would wish, like dolls.
Saint Francis, obligingly revealing his stigmata, revels
in a more intellectual company than that of twittering
birds; Jerome ceases to frown over his book, seeming
almost ready to snub his royal companion
as he scourges himself to give a more competitive
account of his mettle.

In the ambience of athletic, perspiring martyrs
brandishing their assorted arrows, grills, stones,
Catherine reveals herself to be an outrageously
competent mathematician.
Instead of praying devoutly, she wistfully fabricates designs
conjured into being with the aid of a compass, lively entertainments
only to be materialised with wholesome, unfractured wheels.
This is, after all, planned as a holiday for the saints.
The Holy Virgin is surely permitted
to relax the prescribed arcs of her mantle,
vigorously to shake the awakening child
as he reaches out for the apple,
and whisper in St Anne's ear that, truth to tell,
she frequently finds old Joseph.... very .... tedious.

You, my friends who pander to the weakness of your saints,
as you genuflect before the Holy Trinity and the rest,
spare a moment's thought for me, Coco the Contortionist,

so often maligned by you as coarse and misshapen…
a good-for-nothing drawing attention to himself
by mimicking the poses of some Japanese wrestler.
Good friends, like you, I am what I am, a random
ripped-off root from stock of Adam's apple tree.
Carved by a blind artist with a dull knife
in a season of hunger for meaning,
I wish only to hide from your sight
this bruised, bitterwood stump of a rib, which,
believe it or not, as it pleases your worships,
once shielded a live, raw-red
pumping heart.

OUR MADS

Our astounding, abounding, regular town mads
confound us with the hiatus of their presence.
We regard them with white, sepulchred eyes, afraid to see.

Gracious Harry, billboard for Christ, distributes his leaflets
with a special smile for those he senses
are unbelievers.
Duttybwoy hurls threats at his cracked reflection
in the half-boarded up window of a cosy restaurant,
like most everyone in the town, gone bust.
The flippers of champion skinny-dipper Myra
grotesquely overshadow the debris at pavement level.
Her bold breast strokes
no longer evoke a response from the street vendors.
"Is so she like to swim, most times she naked,"
comment the placid police.

We are shamed by the multifarious choked screams
of these aliens behind their masks.
As indifference and disrespect encounter
indifference and disfavour...
We retreat.

My dear fellow aliens,
let us drink to our solidarity.
To the business people of the town I too am a crackpot.

ROCKSTONE! I TOO HAVE LIVED IN ARCADIA!

(For David)

Do not disregard the exclamation mark
that registers the colour of the word
as we Jamaicans understand it.
Ironpressed with dutty it is the currency
of stonebreakers whose daughters may be
today's sophisticated money-managers, or carefree artists.
Born in a small house in St Mary which my father
named Arcadia, having financed its building week by week
in cash earned by giving injections to combat yaws,
I loved the mahogany panelling in the drawing room,
and the grapevine on the front verandah,
its walls etched with the elegant design of imaginary cutstone.
My heart swallowed the centrefold of the sun
that flooded the house from west to east
when I came skipping in from an afternoon romp;
or from a lesson in distinguishing
weeds from plants which must be spared.

My first weekend home from boarding school
was wrecked by the news that the house had been sold
and we were about to leave our Arcadia.
Loss of the barbecue and the slope out back
to the bamboo-fringed pond was almost too much to bear.
Nine years I had been so happy nestled –
come to think of it in retrospect – in a midway Arcadia
tipped off casually by a road that ran its countryman's course
laughing and winking between Gayle
and – would you believe it? – Lucky Hill.
Children are too busy to look back.
Six years flew by like three in our Brown's Town home,
Richmond Villa, once an inn and so sprawling
it had a whole world of unused rooms downstairs
which one could appropriate as an enchanted studio-kingdom.

It had also a ghost in residence who coughed,
oleanders at the windows and trees one could climb.
In the corner of the garden my father made a fish pool
shaped like a heart.

Next, at last, came our own home – the Hillside,
pioneered out of a stony pasture in the year the declaration of war
shunted the big, cruel world into our consciousness.
But what was real was native red earth and rockstone.
Jackass say the road not level.
I had my pubescent awakening to PROBLEMS,
still there was family happiness galore.
My doctor father, a landscape gardener by avocation,
with no public water supply to count on,
carved out a garden that plant lovers came miles to see.
And when he planted Stonehaven for retirement years
at the foot of the Hillside, you can be sure the planning continued;
the rampant garden acquired more drystone walls
and terraces and steps and angled footpaths
than any sensible and busy medical man
would have dared to undertake.

When you visit my Stonehaven of today with its three studios
you will recognise from this compressed life story
the rockstone passion of a Jamaican country bumpkin
born and nurtured in Arcadia.

MY HOUSE

Is this grilled box with a front door some sort of trap?
I live in a personal space
where anything can happen
except that surely God's roof
will not fall on my head.
I am convinced that my house
is set on a firm foundation.
WHAT WAS THAT RUMBLING SOUND I HEARD?
In nineteen-o-seven my father heard
a similar crepitation
and found himself searching the darkness
for something identifiable as sky.
Somehow he managed to clamber out of the fissure
that had received him as an honoured guest.
About fifteen years later he lived to beget me –
A k a (as of today) – respectfully – Miss G.

IN MY HOUSE THE VERY CHAIRS TALK

I pay attention to the voices
of the old furniture in my house.
Suddenly a stately marble-pedestaled bureau mirror
may turn on me with a scowl,
reiterating a rebuke I winced at as a teenager.
Or a self-important mahogany armchair
may akimbo its elbows in a petulant gesture,
informing me that its ample seat with refined straw matting
needs no silly cushion, thank you very much.
When I stoop creakily to whisk the cobwebs
from the underside of a rocker so often evergreened
its surface has the patina of glass, I count my blessings.
Why? – because that sturdy, rustic frame
silently transmits a reassuring message.
Once a verandah chair, it misses the old scenery, maybe,
and the family; but loyal to this
perverse, solitary, aging person
it still rehearses in the tiny breeze
the grilled window allows indoors
the rhythm of a long bygone lullaby.
It tells of what seemed once a potential infinity of contentment,
and of swift, unspoken reconciliations
of so much more that the winds of time
keep under their wings.
So would the rhythm of this rocker and its partner
end a quarrel between imperfect beings – man and wife –
craftily fashioned by the same carpenter.

ISLAND

My land is an island.
My island is a dirty marketplace.
My island is a spinster lady
with a doorknob of hair and a querulous nose.
My I – land is a human body laid out
and waiting for reincarnation
as a nightingale.

LETTER LEFT ON MY DESK BY GILBERT

Greetings, dear sister. Here's to a festive season spent
rethinking the landscape with your brush!
As you know, it was the whiskers
of Grandpappy Hurricane that brushed your cheek.
I left a few green kisses on the panes
of your studio windows as a memento of my frolic.
Apologies for the single window-frame that swelled
and jammed because of my brainstorm.
Long before it shrinks to normal
you'll be busy as usual, I know.
Okay – so I did upend your breadfruit tree,
and snap the trunk of the poinciana.
You must admit that summer bloomer you shot
with your camera had it coming to him.
Must confess I couldn't resist the temptation
to litter the floor of your tidy pasture
with froufrou from the breadnut tree.
Why ever did God make that grand fellow's limbs so brittle?
Forgive! Forgive!
I knew you'd go on working unless the roof blew off
so I spared the roof.
It was the pimento tree the breadfruit brought down
that damaged those zinc sheets you had to replace.
Next to those two fellows the packy dug its toes in
and stood firm. Weren't you relieved?
As one about to wind down till next time,
I salute you, as ever,
sister ever dear to my heart…

old Eye-of-the-Hurricane.

SHELLING GUNGO PEAS

Happiness is
sitting in one's own chair, in one's own living room
and shelling green gungo from one's own backyard tree.
On the low book table to my right I have placed
the broken branches on a newspaper;
there is another newspaper on the floor to catch the debris.
In my lap there is a comely bowl for the chosen ones
and on the table a smaller bowl for the dry peas.
You may not think it, but there are decisions to be made,
for instance, are some of the tiny, sticky ones
too insignificant for admission to Elysium?
Will they blow a breath of green sickness through
tomorrow's rice and peas?
And what of the brownish ones, who seem a bit
too self-contained? Is their special, interior glow
an asset or a liability?
The bowl in my lap fills to overflowing
for the crop is good this year and I have caught it in time.
The fat peas with the brightness and glow of corn grains
seem to appraise their neighbours and say,
you, you and you, it is clear you are still too green,
why, may we ask were you admitted?
As for you, you are as brown as a nut. We don't need you!
And what should I do about the mischievous ones
who insist on rolling under my chair?
Let them lie there, I say, helpless as widow's groats.
More charity may be shown to those who simply nestle
in the mountainous landscape of my person.

Happiness is pouring out the green or greenish globes
measuring cup by measuring cup, the glory of the gleaning.
A pint and a half of tiny worlds flow
shimmering back into the great abyss of the bowl.
The slightly shrivelled ones view the homely ritual

with old wive's grimaces, but no evidence of malice.
As they and I know, from earth they came
and to earth they will return. Willy nilly,
it is they, the despised and rejected,
who are the cupbearers of the future.

THE DOGS

Happiness is
looking into the eyes of a dog who is
faithful but not subservient –
and is better than a horse at cavorting.
He will obey your command to lie down or go O U T
if you insist, but he knows that you can hardly
bear to give the order.
His big clumsy paws resting on your shoulder
may accidentally damage your skin,
but his eyes remind you
that he is your watchman and your friend.
Happiness is
when the wriggly black one
sneaks up into your lap and shifts her body
so she can look into your eyes,
and unadulterated love dulls the usual glint of mischief.
Others have referred to her as the runt of the litter,
but human language reaches her – fortunately –
only in a sloppy transcript. Even so, she recognises her detractors.
Happiness is
eyes which meet yours for a moment as a tail wags
to acknowledge the piece of chicken-back which, after all,
makes life's daily mound of stodgy cornmeal quite....
... worthwhile

BIBLIOMANIA

Happiness is
books, books and more books
and a special room with bookshelves
you can dignify with the name of "library";
art books, beautiful to handle,
some with colour plates tipped in –
but never mind if they aren't,
or if some of the illustrations are only in b & w;
books so numerous one could not possibly live long enough
to read, let alone reread them all!
Crashing like an elephant through one
leads to tiptoing through six more.
How could one ever be alone with such company!

Thank you all you writers of books,
and publishers, and booksellers.
Who could grudge you the cash-in-hand compensation
of the "bottom line"?
Blessed be friends who give books as presents
and select the titles like posies for a bridal bouquet.
Oh, you dear fellow bibliophiles,
how proud I am to have my own name set in type as curator
to one small, curious assemblage of words!

One of these days I'm going to get myself
swallowed by a book, and I shan't mind at all
if the pages are of shine-eye quality,
with no inclination to curl and go limp in damp weather.

Please God, let my purgatory be passed
in some aromatic tome
fresh-minted by art book publishers
justly proud of their discriminating author.
(let us say, a Georges de la Tour monograph)

May the author disclose to me – with modest fanfare – all or some
of the painter's personal foibles, and expose
the chequered provenance of his dubiously authenticated works
like a clean, going-out-to-dine shirt laid out for scrutiny.

Pressed for time, like baby's breath fern
between the pages
of God's good book, is the bibliomaniac.
Who can deny that Jonah within the maw of his leviathan

experienced a similar ecstasy!

STILL LIFE WITH CROCUSES

(by a Dutch Artist)

Four purple crocuses in a ceramic bowl
lift their heads clear of the kitchen clutter
and unclench their spirits; the salt solitude
of their bulbs nurtured from infancy
by invasive tides begins to freshen.
Springtime in the garden beyond the window
rims and rhymes with light every humble artefact.

The regal purple of the crocuses blanches the beholder,
dispensing a threat, a darkness beyond the russet
halfway to extinction,
but in this moment of epiphany – who cares?
Halved and quartered for its meridian sweetness
a golden orange on a plate bares its chest to the sunlight
and, half shadowed, emits a glare.
Where it came from, tidal waves of crocuses, yellow and white,
rise up after the first shower no matter what the season.
It is enough for them that without forethought or afterthought
they gulp the air with the raindrops, and celebrate the sun.

POOR MAN'S ORCHID

My struggle to communicate with you
is no more than a pencil drawing
of a piece of Nature that by tomorrow
will have almost faded from memory.
The magenta that pulses in this flower
demands but wisely resists capture.
Put away your watercolour set, my dear.
It will serve no useful purpose.

LOST AND FOUND

(i)
Dark page of hair bobbing in the wind,
a boy of fourteen or so walks downwind,
studying the ground his eyes do not see.
He does not know I exist.
He strides through the dark pages of my thoughts,
his long brown hands
cautiously pocketed.

(ii)
In a field where packages of rice
are doled out at the turnstile – along with tickets,
there are too many people.
Some must do without rations for the picnic.
I hand over mine to a stranger who seems lost
without a handout... and return
to the sweet solitude of my studio.

(iii)
Now they are assembling
strange mechanical contrivances
so the minibuses can hold
more baskets – and people.
Everyone is looking for something deposited somewhere.
Will the topheavy bus make it round the ill-fated bend
or tumble like a bug over the precipice?
It is too late to choose
not to take one's seat for the journey.

(iv)
In this maze of darkened streets
I have mislaid my car as usual,
quite forgotten where I parked it.
(And never did memorize the licence number.)
Has anyone seen a straying Lynx Escort

sand coloured and discreet?
Wrong lane, wrong colour,
wrong side of street for the hour.
Driving the very car for which I'm searching,
I'm frantic for directions.
What is the name of this street?
Does it lead to the intersection
where I dropped off my driver?
Young man found in a tangle of cards
he is faceless as any untitled club member
in a standard pack.
One-way streets with no signs,
turnings announced by orchestrated sighs.
Signals more confusing than the twinkling eyes
of the plain spread out below in this lonely ascent
to the top of a world named Stony Hill.
Here one could choose to roll over the edge
and meet no more persons
to question or be questioned by.

SHARING A JOKE

Share with me the open secret
That it is no joke to be old,
that it is not true
people are as old as they feel.
I am an old woman, a young girl and a child.
It is no joke to be three people
who don't quite understand one another.
Your sharing of the comedy
will light up the darkness of my long travail.

SPACED IN

Thoughts that follow the wayward moon
turn wispy.
Barefoot spirits yearn for hard, cold floors,
and kick aside the scatter rugs.
There is no charted course
through history's mysteries.
Balls of fluff encumber the graph paper leagues
of interminable space.

BRAINBUSTED

There are so many loose words
clattering around in this ancient box
labelled "If found afloat return to G.E."
that the hubris of their meanings elbowing each other
is like a tempest tearing its hair
within the confines of a tiny shell.
"Be quiet there, you antiquarian and tedious mutts!
Do you think ink ink ink you are persons of consequence
just because you bark in sequence?"

A PIECE OF HAND EMBROIDERY

I was only need, need, needling
you a little; the red stain
on the fine linen clasped in the ring
of the embroidery frame is no more than
a dramatisation of the fabric's texture.
It was my hand, not yours, that directed the needle.
The stain is composed of my heart's blood, not yours.
Where were you when my hand slipped?
You were far away, perhaps you never existed.
I have discarded that piece of unfinished work.
It is time to get on with my love letter to the world,
which may be as torrid as a Gauguin landscape
or spin itself out in an abstract border
of the sort that wreathes itself round all aliens and isolates
till they die, or live silently screaming
from the agony of imminent exposure.

WASHDAY

It is time for the stretching of lines –
not words strung out at random
but corded simplicities arranged
so they ripple
when the slightest breeze
tugs at their bellying certainties,
or tickles the stitched monogram
in the pocket of a pinafore.
Lay the more chastened garments
on the stones to dry,
but remember to take them in
before the sun eats holes
through to the chastity
that once they guarded.

STOWAWAY

Hunched in the hold,
he ignores the swatch of liberated turquoise
at his back
and projects the future
from behind his own
white-rimmed, impenetrable darkers;
the tote bag at his feet
carries all he thinks he will need.
It is empty.
Sweat soaked ganzies,
tatters of a thousand indignities,
have been left behind
along with the ancient fetishes.
They belong to his discarded world –
or so he thinks –
stepping out from his inner darkness.
Like a born-again Myal Columbus
he is all set to launch his potency
after a majestic landfall.

MALICE AFORETHOUGHT

Girl, I going to ask you to do me a favour –
though you don't know me
and probably he has never mentioned my name.
If – or when – you decide you fed up with him,
and is time to leave him, do it with style.
Don't bother with words, they don't carry no meaning
with such a lightweight as that one.
Just focus you eyes on that shiny dome
with the few mouse-grey stragglers draped across it.
Never mind how people say baldness is a sign of virility,
is young guys they referring to, and anyway
there are other things besides this macho machine
as you know, my dear.
Wait till you see him put up one hand to stroke
the brazen globe, and look sideways, as if he thinking,
that last one was too old, maybe this one too forceripe!
Is high time he find out in crop-over time
the field not greening for second spring.
When you see him take out his glasses and polish them,
and squint at you sort of sideways
as if is you make him feel the years
crawling all over him like chink,
don't say a word, you hear, darling.
Just turn you back on him and walk out.
Do it so quietly him don't even hear
the door shut behind you.

MISS ROSE-OF-THE-WORLD CUCHIE

"Speak to us, Miss Cuchie," plead the schoolgirls,
prim and graceful in their uniforms,
"We hardly know what it is like to be us;
what is it like to be you?"

Miss Cuchie, the two-headed rag doll, knows
that two heads are better than one.
She and the schoolgirls share the silence of accomplices.
The rocks they will have to clamber over,
she has had to find a way over or round.

Miss Rose-of the-world Cuchie,
with your two heads, one black, one white,
which would you rather have tucked under your skirt
in an emergency?
You Jamaican Miss Cuchies of tomorrow, all you
mothers, caring spinsters and lady-teachers,
don't ever let the Rude Boys get away
with calling any of you "mule".
That red rose emblazoned on your skirt ,
Miss Cuchie, shames the spoiled males of the present generation.
Do better, young girls,
when it comes to raising
the next generation of boy children!

INCENDIARIES

What absurd aberration of the human mind
propelled that de-orbited astronaut
(whose name evades my memory)
into a race for the U.S. presidency?
Why should Art Deco painter Tamara de Lempicka,
having watched her skill and her pizzaz fade with age,
demand of a faithful friend
that he dust Popocatepetl with her ashes?
Incendiarists all, we seek to light a flame
to perpetuate our candle glow.
"Tell all mourners," wrote Langston Hughes
in a pre-prepared memorial service poem,
"to mourn in red – cause there ain't no sense
in my bein' dead."
How pathetically we impose our futile gestures
on friends, hangers on, next of kin!
My ashes, scattered on this rural hillside I have loved,
will not suffice to nurture a blade of grass
nor secure it from almost certain take over
by squatterdom.

CASSIA YELLOW

How should we react
to this late September
declaration of rectitude?
Such astringent yellow
shawled in comfortable dark green
demotivates every drought-harassed
neighbourhood tree,
bush or spear of grass.
October rains are taking their time
to pierce and shatter
the self-possession of the rainclouds.
The season's apprehensive attendants
find no relief in sighs
or ticking off dates with the pertinacity
of peenie wallies.
A few yards from my window
a nondescript, barely hanging-in-there
vine on a wire fence
halfmasts a yellowing leaf.
Nature's mysteries
begrudge us the satisfaction
of easy explanations.

LEFT HAND, RIGHT HAND

I obey the instructions of my left hand.
If it says to my right hand,
"Get busy, set your five artisans to work,
drawing out the secrets of your soul
in a language that others may read",
it does its best; though that may fall far short
of the intention of the left-behind, intuitive self.
Even so, the left seems to understand
that it is wise to keep many secrets,
otherwise the totality of being
could not survive the shock of exposure to itself.

WHY YEARN TO BE A BUTTERFLY ?

Its limited talent and volition
clamped like its jaws
to the objective of metamorphosis,
the caterpillar surely exults in its efficiency.
The butterfly alights on a petal
and nervously palpitates its wings.
Where else has it in mind to go
but from this fragile world to another?
Perhaps it sees its own reflection
in the exotic, creased landing stage,
and senses the shadow of some huge predator
hovering overhead.

REVOLT OF THE THIRD ESTATE OF EXPRESSIVE WILL

When no boy syllables come tumbling out,
lighting each other like firecrackers,
should one sit and mourn silently,
or wail beyond the hearing of banshee-folk,
astonishing even one's self
with the absence of alliterative consonance?

There is a time for patching what age and use have ripped,
and a time for silent brooding. But best of all is the time
of rising with the sun-shocked sky
that silhouettes early birds clattering in the trees,
for awareness of Nature's glory brings those
irrepressible boys back, eager as ever for a raid.
Arise! Arise! Set down the country words in whatever order
the bird-like notes arrange themselves!

I CONFRONT MY TASKMASTER

My taskmaster scowls down at me as usual
and points an arthritic forefinger,
directing his wrath at an unfinished sketch.
"Who do you think you are, for God's sake?" he asks.
"Methuselah lived nine hundred sixty and nine years
before he got to walk with God,
and that was seven hundred eighty and two years
beyond the hundred and eighty-seventh
in which he begat Lamech.
Who are you to opt out at a mere seventy-two
and leave one of these puny children of yours
not even half-conceived on the drawing board?"

"Old man, you have grown hunchbacked
from looking down at me" – this is what I think but daren't say.
"Others nowadays retire at sixty-five –
some women, I believe, at sixty.
Why pick on this poor-me spinster
who has no blood heirs but these paper beings?
Yesterday it was the word processor
that gorged itself on my energies,
today you burden me with images
that call for paint brushes.
Do your foreign gods not instruct
you in mercy to the aged?"

Ultimately all commands come from the One and Only.
He instructs me and insists that my mission,
whatever it may be, must be fulfilled.
Thank you, All Knowing, for providing a taskmaster
who keeps my eyes bright and my step somewhat springy
at age seventy and two.

JOURNEYMAN DUNKLEY
A TRIBUTE

John Dunkley was the offspring of cultures
eager to mate. The drums of Africa
and the hunting horns of Europe cohabited in his veins.
He populated the drab cornices of Jamaican Victoriana,
formal as palm leaf fans at an Anglican service for the dead,
with creatures that rustled in the twilight.
His inexplicable rosettes laid out in tidy garden beds
hid secrets of crab and jerboa, of carapace and horn and scale
from a continent of darkness
his respectable neighbours preferred to deride.
Restless as water, as a youth he lost – and found – himself
in the wildwoods of central America.
But Jamaica drew him back because to him it was home.
The loggerhead and chic-me-chic, and sewi sewi and Auntie Katie
provided a chorus of welcome.
He took to paintbrush and chisel, and they released his dreams.
To him the grand waterfalls and canyons he had seen
back-lit the humbler green gorge of the Rio Cobre.

Icarus plunged dramatically to his doom.
Dunkley lived out the allotment of his journeyman's days
in his own backyard – and ours.
Every day he studied the streets of Kingston
as he journeyed to his barber shop.

Sure-footed as a mule, Dunkley
whittled for his amusement one day a dray.
Two draymen, tiny and ordinary as sunlight,
take their responsibility
for the casks, and the uprearing of the fractious beasts –

seriously.

To Dunkley life was a comic interlude,
a family joke

with echoes in the crypt.

WILD WORDS

I thought I was wild
with caring for a person.
I was wild
to write a poem
saying I was wild with caring.
Having written it, I am caring –
but for whom I really don't know.
The wild wind
has died down to a rustle.
An invisible John-to-whit
prepares to have his say.
"Sweet John, John, sweet John-to whit!"
The folk of old
who translated his self-centred refrain
showed their good sense
in such country matters.
Who but the most foolish of old crones
would be cozened
by such a Jamaican charmer?
Now that the ways of human beings
are writ large for me
in sight-saving print for the bookish elderly,
Spring may still prove to be a trying time,
in the garden,
in my cultivated, caring,
aged heart.

OTHER RECENT POETRY BY JAMAICAN AUTHORS FROM PEEPAL TREE

Geoffrey Philp

HURRICANE CENTER

El niño stirs clouds over the Pacific. Flashing tv screens urge a calm that no one believes. The police beat a slouched body, crumpled like a fist of kleenex. The news racks are crowded with stories of pestilence, war and rumours of war. The children, once sepia-faced cherubim, mutate to monsters that eat, eat, eat. You notice a change in your body's conversation with itself and in the garden the fire ants burrow into the flesh of the fruit.

Geoffrey Philp's poems stare into the dark heart of a world where hurricanes, both meteorological and metaphorical, threaten you to the last cell. But the sense of dread also reveals what is most precious in life, for the dark and the accidental are put within the larger context of season and human renewal and *Hurricane Center* returns always to the possibilities of redemption and joy.

In the voices of Jamaican prophets, Cuban exiles, drunks, race-track punters, canecutters, rastamen, middle-class householders and screw-face ghetto sufferers, Geoffrey Philp writes poetry which is both intimately human and cosmic in scale. On the airwaves between Miami and Kingston, the rhythms of reggae and mambo dance through these poems.

Geoffrey Philp was born in Jamaica. He now lives and works in Miami. He is the author of *Florida Bound* and a collection of short stories, *Uncle Obadiah and the Alien*, also published by Peepal Tree.

69 pages £6.99 ISBN 1-900715-23-6 1998

Ralph Thompson

MOVING ON

The poems in *Moving On* recreate moments of change, loss and epiphany. There are vivid glimpses of a prewar Jamaican childhood – of sexual discovery under a billiard table and of the rude ingratitude of a goat saved from dissection in the school biology lab. The long sequence, 'Goodbye Aristotle, So Long America' explores the years of study at a Jesuit University in America and the making both of a lifetime's values and of the sense of irony which has made it possible to sustain them.

Other poems reflect on the experience of ageing, dealing not only with its increasing vulnerabilities, but also with its increased appreciation for what nurtures the survival of human relationships through time.

Jamaica is ever present in these poems, a place of aching natural beauty whose violent energies can only be viewed with an ambivalent love and fear, where:

In the city's bursting funeral parlours
the corpses glow at night, nimbus of blue
acetylene burning the darkness under the roof,
lighting the windows... crunch of bone and sinew
as a foot curls into a cloven hoof.

Louis Simpson described Ralph Thompson's first collection, also published by Peepal Tree, *The Denting of a Wave*, as "First rate poetry... intelligent and gifted with a sense of humour" and other reviewers praised its warmth, exact observation, craft and vivid storytelling. These qualities are present to an enhanced degree in *Moving On*.

Ralph Thompson is a Jamaican who, as well as being a painter and a poet, is the Senior Executive of on his country's biggest companies.

72 pages £6.99 ISBN 1-900715-17-1 1998

Kwame Dawes

SHOOK FOIL

When the guitars tickle a bedrock of drum and bass, when the girl a shock out and a steady hand curve round her sweat-smooth waist, when the smell of *Charlie* mingles with the chemicals of her hair and the groove is of the sweetest friction… how is a young man to keep his way pure?

Kwame Dawes' poetry rises to new heights in these psalms of confession and celebrations of reggae's power to prophesy, to seek after righteousness and seduce the body and mind. Here is poetry walking the bassline, which darts sweetly around the rigid lick of the rhythm guitar yet expressing all the sadness and alienation at the heart of reggae. This, for Dawes, is the earth which 'never tells me my true home' and where behind every *chekeh* of the guitar there is the ancestral memory of the whip's crack.

Shook Foil dramatises the conflict between the purity of essences and the taints of the actual, not least in the poems which focus on Bob Marley's life. Here is the rhygin, word-weaving prophet *and* the philanderer with the desperate hunger for yard pumpum, the revealer of truths *and* the buffalo soldier who has married yard with show biz affluence.

Above all there is the intense sadness of Marley's death, for how can one live without the duppy conqueror's defiant wail in an island gone dark for the passing of his song?

But for *Shook Foil* there is always the gospeller's hope that the dead will rise from dub ruins and patch a new quilt of sound for the feet to prance on. And when the high hat shimmering and the bass drum thumping, what else to do but dance?

Kwame Dawes is the author of four other collections of poetry: *Progeny of Air*, *Prophets*, *Jacko Jacobus* and *Requiem*, published by Peepal Tree.

75 pages £6.99 ISBN 1-900715-14-7 1997

Anthony McNeill

CHINESE LANTERNS FROM THE BLUE CHILD

Somebody is hanging:
a logwood tree
laden with blossoms
in a deep wood.
The body stirs left
in the wind;
If the wind could send
its miracle breath
back to that person,
I tell you it would.
Love is Earth's mission
despite the massed dead.
On the night of the hanging
the Autumn moon bled.

Anthony McNeill was without doubt amongst the finest contemporary Caribbean poets, whose previous collections, *Reel from 'The Life Movie'* and *Credences at the Altar of Cloud,* were hailed as works of immense originality. *Chinese Lanterns from the Blue Child* won the 1995 Jamaican National Literary Award. Completed shortly before his death, it is a farewell to the world which moves like a bird in flight between moments of painful regret, wry humour and a sense of closure.

Anthony McNeill's word-lanterns will continue to flame in the darkness long beyond his death. He was born in Jamaica in 1941. He died in 1996.

56 pages £5.99 ISBN 1-900715-18-X 1998

Peepal Tree Press publishes a wide selection of outstanding fiction, poetry, drama, history and literary criticism with a focus on the Caribbean, Africa, the South Asian diaspora and Black life in Britain. Peepal Tree is now the largest independent publisher of Caribbean writing in the world. All our books are high quality original paperbacks designed to stand the test of time and repeated readings.

All Peepal Tree books should be available through your local bookseller, though you are most welcome to place orders direct with us. When ordering a book direct from us, simply tell us the title, author, quantity and the address to which the book should be mailed. Please enclose a cheque or money order for the cover price of the book, plus 75p towards postage and packing.

Peepal Tree produces a yearly catalogue which gives current prices in sterling, US and Canadian dollars and full details of all our books. Write, phone or fax for your free copy.

You can contact Peepal Tree direct at:

17 King's Avenue
Leeds LS6 1QS
United Kingdom

tel: 44 (0)113 245 1703
fax: 44 (0)113 246 8368
e-mail hannah@peepal.demon.co.uk